Rafting on the Water Table

Rafting
ON THE WATER TABLE

Poems by Susan Steger Welsh

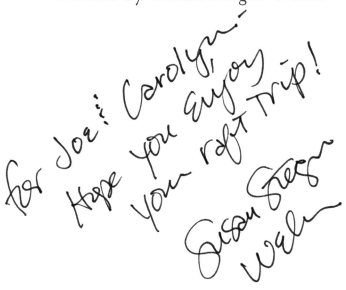

For Joe & Carolyn—
Hope you Enjoy
your raft Trip!

Susan Steger
Welsh

Minnesota Voices Project Number 96
New Rivers Press 2000

© 2000 by Susan Steger Welsh

First Edition

Library of Congress Control Number: 99-68467

ISBN: 0-89823-202-3

Edited by Connie Wanek

Book design and typesetting by Percolator

Printed in the United States of America

New Rivers Press is a nonprofit literary press dedicated to publishing emerging writers.

The publication of *Rafting on the Water Table* has been made possible by generous grants from the Jerome Foundation and from Target Foundation on behalf of Dayton's, Mervyn's California, and Target Stores.

This activity is made possible in part by a grant provided by the Minnesota State Arts Board, through an appropriation by the Minnesota State Legislature. In addition, this activity is supported in part by a grant from the National Endowment for the Arts.

Additional support has been provided by the General Mills Foundation, the McKnight Foundation, the Star Tribune Foundation, and the contributing members of New Rivers Press.

MINNESOTA
STATE ARTS BOARD

NATIONAL
ENDOWMENT
FOR THE
ARTS

New Rivers Press
420 North Fifth Street Suite 1180
Minneapolis, MN 55401

www.newriverspress.org

Contents

One

Two

Three

In memory of my mother

One

In Defense of Semicolons

As a child I had no use for them,
preferring instead the firm
grip of conjunctions, the certainty
of the full stop, the way
commas can stall
a bedtime.
A master poet says
don't use them; they're ugly.
You have to admire a man
who'll take a stand
on punctuation.
But how else
can you keep the family together?
Some things want to move
slowly; a dash would be wrong.
Not the smear of rain on a windshield,
but a snowflake in the palm
of a parent's glove.
The world is full
of lists, and commas give way
under pressure. The homely semicolon
holds, a full moon floating
above the ocean's chop,
the undertow of history, waves
of events separated
by breath—my breath, your breath,
it doesn't matter.
As a child,
I would have given everything
for beauty, but I'm past that.
Now I can see how much hinges
on punctuation, the small
clear marks we use to find our place.

Swimming Lessons

1.

In my Mother's Day gift book
How Much I Love My Mama
my ten-year-old lists the usual, and then—
I love my Mama more than a fish loves water.
Green seaweeds awash in blue,
a purple fish who says *I love water*
in a yellow bubble.
Don't fish assume water?
Can it be his soul remembers
floating in me?
Does it occur to the fish
there is an end to water?

I see myself an ocean,
wave rippled spine
holding back
the sky chasm.

2.

Her questions come from the backseat,
or across the table, as I witness
history's slowest recorded consumption of peas.

Mama, how is fourteen a number?
What happens
to the whale bodies when they die—
do they just pile up
on the bottom of the ocean?
Why doesn't the glue stick
inside the tube?
Do you ever wonder
if it's really night
and you're just dreaming?

And then in bed, just before
the waves of sleep
close over her head:
Mama,
how long
is day?

3.
The bubbles have softened her up,
soaked off our fight earlier that day.
She offers to take down
the *I Hate Mom* signs taped up in her room,
even the one adding: *I Mean It.*
Nice touch, her brother had grinned at dinner.

4.
The children are so
small inside their needs.
They can barely see
over the top. My son
inside his smooth ten-year-old body
comes to announce his hunger,
confident I will fill it. He doesn't
see mine.

5.
On the shore together we learn that water
won't be refused.

The hands of my children
scoop and smooth mounds of sand
but always a few grains slide backwards.
Each pat calls forth
its own washing away.

The hands of the waves
play scales in the sand
over and over and never
the same twice.

6.
You take them to swimming lessons
so they learn to float
above their fear, how long it's safe to hold
their breath. You try to make them buoyant
and wise. You teach them to look always

for the things seen only by squinting, to notice
when the earth opens and offers things
and to heed the river songs,
the ones that tell how rivers die
daily into the life of oceans.
It is the oceans
that store the heat,
send the storms.

Empty Nest

1.
The surprising strength of a frail thing,
remnant of hornet or wasp, the tenants
evicted by winter. This paper-thin thunder
of tunnels, a home to creatures who buzz,
lurk in cans of soda to sting our tongues.
You had tunnels like this,
that went inward and stopped,
like gloves for a thousand flown-away fingers,
which never could grasp
what you wanted. Tunnels thin,

like the walls of a bedroom
where you fought with Dad when you thought
we were sleeping. Your anger
when he disappeared on weekends
with waders and a grin. The blue bills
and pheasants which hung, crimp-necked
in the garage, until he melted wax and coated them,
stripped the feathers off in laundry tubs,
giving me wings I thought were beautiful.
I spread them and ran through your house.

2.
When your circle was closing,
and the nurses couldn't please you,
we brought you back home.
I tried to be what you wanted,
make you brave with pills
nested in plastic trays
on the kitchen table.

Was it inspiring, that you could talk
about music for the funeral?
I was thinking of how the house smelled
when you cooked the game
he brought. *Damnduck*
you called it, one stinging word,
served with wine and wild rice,
the color of emptiness,
brown sinking to shadow.

Spiders Keep House

Sleep is the gift of spiders.
CARL SANDBURG

I envy those spiders,
how they set their tables and wait,
disguise themselves as centerpieces.
Tonight, as I wait in a cabin for sleep,
I cannot find the center of anything.

The night is blind, as spiders are.
I pick my way carefully
through sounds that bang at the screen:
a breeze, sweet breath of forest.
Creatures scrambling leaves.
Shrieks and shufflings—a lull.
My mother, crouching in the pine cones,
speaking Polish, trying to explain to God
why I never dream about her.
Not once in nineteen years. Overhearing this,

I feel again her hands toweling me dry
after a bath. She brushes my hair straight,
tells me what a good father I have, that I must
be good, too, since God was holding her
accountable for my still-damp soul.

I spend years slipping out of the clothes she dressed me in.

In families and in cabins, cobwebs
hold up the corners. Their ruins
float like chiffon scarves, the ghostly wave
of the mothers who made them, spiders
who breathed softly through their stomachs

and made plans at night, working patiently
to repair the damage of the day, their webs
knit of holes, strong silk
knotted around the empty places.

The spiderlings wake up to find
their mothers gone. They let the wind pull
the silk out, follow the tug
into the drop and sway,

into the center of their lives.

Atheist Madalyn Murray O'Hair
May Never Come Back

Newspaper headline, September 1996

When a person is seventy-seven and mean as spit,
proud of being the Most Hated Woman in America,
always shoving back
in your face every outlandish thing
some dreamer once wrote about freedom,
you tend not to miss her. When she goes on vacation
and never comes back, you take your time
getting up a search party.
                    It's been over
a year now. When Madalyn Murray O'Hair
fails to show up to picket the pope,
it's time to consider the possibilities.
Atheists don't like
to take anything on faith, but they begin to say
they don't expect her back. Perhaps she is exhausted,
hoarse from preaching unbelief. A spokesman
says her disappearance is atheism's first mystery.
Says, *Who knows? Maybe she was taken bodily
into heaven.*
                    Picture this instead:
Madalyn Murray O'Hair out walking the moonfallen
crests of Wyoming where, if there were
a Second Coming, it could not sneak up on you.
Madalyn Murray O'Hair fishing in streams
where the trout are attached to their shadows.
Madalyn Murray O'Hair drinking in bars
full of men in boots and sleeveless undershirts,
where the regulars complain about the futility
of waiting for something to save you:
                    a woman, rain,
compromise with some damn environmentalist.
In Wyoming, there are miles
and miles of blond, crewcut hills that never
knew shade, buildings that never knew paint.

Ranchers' houses sit like fists slammed into dirt,
surrounded by every piece of equipment
that ever broke or wore out, held together
by rust and a certain grim determination,
as if it wants to be around to say,
                    I told you so.
Around here, being too certain of the wrong thing can kill you,
sure as the wind'll come whipping out of the west,
carve canyons that prove history is just a whole
lot of stuff that never got swept up and went bad in layers.
                    Why would she
come back? Better to lie low in the mountains,
where snow has the grit to hang on. When you give up your life
for something, you do not let go its hand. Not even
when your grip has gone to bone.

Still Standing

We fly past them
on the highway through Wisconsin,
all the falling-down farm buildings.
I want to sketch or take pictures,
but we never stop. Theirs
is the splendid architecture
of collapse, the languid curve
of sway-backed ceiling, walls
barely standing, an impossibly
parallel leaning. Roof planks
peeled back or missing,
as if the sheds were rising,
groggy and unsteady,
from disheveled beds,
to stagger through tall grass.

In an old barn that's now a gallery
in Door County, we circle, arms
behind our backs,
gazing at the framed questions
of artists. Here, a photograph, titled
Growing Old Together.
A tree, half bare,
and a weathered farm building,
bracing each other's
decline. *Which do you want to be?*
I ask, and he answers
without hesitation: *The house.*

A certain amount of rain,
enough wind with sand in its fist,
the tireless track of sun.
Wood's grain rises,
bleached and splintered.
Not sad but noble, this kneeling,
this slow surrender,
this plain
and steadfast love.

Widow

Since his death she plants only trees:
white oak, blue spruce, balsam fir.
She is raising shadows,
wants to see how they pace the yard,
overtaking, then relinquishing
the lawn he tended,
cycling long,
short, long—
a requiem in Morse code.
    Next year, or

the year after, she says,
sunflowers. Something reckless,
gaudy, trained on light.

Great Blue Heron

Meditative, calm as an undertaker,
the stroll all silk, as if choreographed

to chant. Two or three feathers
lift like incense into the breeze. He lands,

as if by accident, behind the old woman fishing.
As if he lent that fish to her, he scoops it up casually,

holds it motionless in his beak, as if
momentarily distracted by some unremembered

happiness. Later, he makes
his wide-toed way across the lawn, stares

through screens into dark rooms where we wait,
amazed at what nerve can get you.

In a Motel in Custer,
South Dakota

The coffee in this town is thin
as mountain air, but I am wide
awake after our walk and the sight
of Custer's name in lights,
a curious marquee branded high
on the hillside's pine hide.

The bed is strange.
I take the side with the lamp
to read, and you roll grumbling
that we're on the wrong sides.
When I curl next to you, complete
the quotation mark, you complain.
Your arm doesn't know how to hug me
from that side. I laugh
and hope to distract you from this,
but I lose you
to the time zone change,
the hours on the road.
I was making other plans
for your hands, but already they fall open,
release the steering wheel, miles
of new country. My eyes close,
see again the eerie braille of traffic
signs rushing out of the woods,
the map folded in my lap
as we negotiate high curves.

Outside, across the road,
mountain shrinks slowly,
imperceptibly from sky.
This has been going on
for years.

The Best Thing about the Wind

is the way it plays around. How wind
toys with dust and drops it, waltzes shirts
hanging out to dry, so they dance,
like goofy scarecrow ghosts. How it lifts the hems
of green things, high-fives the pineconed crowns
of spruce. The wind is always switching,

dropping off, coming up, dying down.
We fall for it every time.

Light moves always at the same speed
but this is not what we want
from wind. On the prairie, where wind
goes into its windup and pelts us
with an unending string of fast balls,
we shield our faces, turn away.
Relentless wind drives us mad.

And when it pouts,
withholds itself, we are uneasy,
like children watching out windows,
waiting for fathers who disappoint.
In the stillness we feel the weight of other things
pressing in. We beg for breeze.

We can stand a tantrum, because we know
the wind will relent. One day
it pummels in fury, then steals away
like the tide, returning later, whispering
kisses, pockets full of shine and sweet.

For frivolous wind,
we open our windows, forgive
everything. We wait,
like lonesome candles,
for a spark from the wind
on its way somewhere else.

Regarding the Discovery
of Two Planets

The astronomers are
beside themselves with joy.
Finally, proof: two stars wobbling,
each pulled off course
by a planet not previously listed
in the program. With stars,
and with people, it is the trembling

which betrays. Who
would have suspected them,
beloved Big Dipper and steady Virgo,
of hiding this news? Stargazers
shiver across a distance

of thirty-five light-years. Thirty-five—
the half-life of a human. Time enough
to get our hands on the question, fling it out
into the universe. Maybe we'll hear back
from cousins on the new planets.

The astronomers say any life there
would form without touching
the ground. But it rains
and the oceans heave
in the amplitude of what is possible
along the tether of gravity.

Grammar in the Kingdom of God

The imagination is not God, but it is the banquet at which we may feast with God.
JAIME MEYER

What I want is a glimpse, a nod,
a touch on the arm. But I cannot even see
where God is. Servants hoist platters

like steaming trophies, run barefoot
past dancers with tambourines,
vendors hawking postcards, beggars

banging bowls. Children spill
into the room like marbles.
I remember what the Jesuit said,

that God isn't big
on clarity; it's bad for business.
So I look for the least likely disguise.

There? The nervous ventriloquist
quoting Cicero? His eyebrows go up
and down like wings caught off-balance,

his thin arms awkward, the voice
of an oboe. One of the dogs?
Inhaling crumbs flung on the floor, angling

for a scratch behind the ears,
badgering for a walk—four-legged
unconditional love. Or perhaps the pitch

of activity is a clue and they're right,
the people who say God is a verb:
singular and plural, regular and irregular,

active and passive. The uncertainty
of subjunctive, when I cannot tell
if something's true, or merely what I

desire. Is God, then, the infinitive?
To roar, to quake, to question?
I conjugate my life uneasily—

first person, second person, third—
a trinity where everything is present,
and nothing perfect.

November Sleeping

To be so late in the year gloveless
makes us giddy. We are out
past curfew, cheating winter.
We deny the daily
subtraction of sun, now shining sideways,
feeling its way along
the gold green hills by heart.
Over our heads
crooked tree fingers stretch,
paw the sky as if to massage
the stiff shoulders of sleep.

Night collects itself early. Yet the wind
is still soft, like your breath on my back
as you sleep. I lie awake
remembering the silky tops of wild grasses
skimming under my hand.

Two

Implosion

In our part of the country,
January shows you how much
is left when everything is gone.
GARRISON KEILLOR

This morning it is seven below. We snap
a down jacket around the video camera,
go out to record the implosion
of the old Montgomery Ward building.
The sun hesitates on the housetops, inhales
the chimney fog, knowing it is both too early
and too late. A helicopter hovers. The siren sounds
and the children forget
their cold feet. The noise
is first: *BOOM BOOM bup bup bup.*
The right shoulder sags, then
the long neck of the tower, and finally
the left shoulder. Smoke and dust
rise up pink but cannot grasp
the hole in the sky. This takes
nine seconds. A child,
the face of wonder tied into a purple hood
cries, *Dad! Look! It's already*
not there! I read
that astronomers believe

the dark-gloved hands holding space open
are mostly stars already not there, suns
collapsed into cold
white dwarves. This takes ten
billion years. We only find them
when they tug
at the hurtling light of other stars, bending
what they cannot stop. On TV I track

the white storm which slips away from us
to fill the veins and valleys of Boston
and Philadelphia and New York. Five inches
an hour rearranges lives, the schedules of planes,
erasing even skyscrapers
over Central Park. This takes
one day. They will grind up

Montgomery Ward, make gravel
for roads, the places where the noise
lives, the places the plows and the shovelers on the news
want to get back to. They can't stand the soft
silence. I want to touch their sleeves, say *Listen*.
This is what it sounds like, the voices
of the disappeared.

Swim the Night

We lean into door frames and look
up, unconscious
of our own revolution, transfixed
    by the tides of stars,
        how they arc inward and out
           leaving behind constellations like
        seashells, cupped
    to the ears of angels.

From the moon we learn fractions
and the making of a new thing
by taking away—
    like haircuts,
    sculpting,
    pruning dead wood.

Moon, they say you have
no light of your own
    —only reflection
like the women
with eyes that follow
and hands that fold.
Women hitched to sons
and fathers of sons.
Moon women
keeping one side
always in darkness.
Women riding
the wheeling earth.

Visiting Aunt Dorothy on Her Birthday

At seventy she quit standing on her head but not,
fourteen years later, telling of it, and telling how she climbed
the water reservoir with her three brothers and then dove,
fearless, into a stream squeezed
between two rocks. How she'd always wanted
to be a gym teacher but had, of course,
not two dimes for schooling. Today
she presses two crisp dollar bills
into the hands of my children, promises my daughter
the porcelain cat she cradles. Aunt Dorothy's arms
circle the room proudly, with its stacks
of birthday cards with Hallmark roses,
and vases of carnations and tulips
standing in front of a fireplace
no longer used. It was always
too crowded for children here,
and now every flat surface is crammed with cut glass
and collectibles given to her by the old women she befriended,
who kept dying and leaving her things. *This,* she says,
picking up one thing after another, *is from my rich friend.*
Names, she says, *that goes.* But she remembers the numbers,
and recites them all, asking us to guess
how much things are worth, showing us
moody landscapes some dealer told her
were valuable and he must know,
he's left Duluth now. She complains about how much
the last bill from her doctor was, but I'm distracted
by her nylon headband, that unreal blue
of October skies in calendars. Her jewelry
is mismatched, and heavy, clanking when she plucks
at my arm as we talk on the sofa, a conversation that careens
from the basement, where 160 hats sleep,
swaddled in tissue, fifteen or twenty to the box,
all collected during her years in retail, gifts, she tells me,
from her buyers; to the attic,
a virtual emporium of bargains too good to pass up:
brooms, boxes of unopened undershirts and shoes in the
size of her late husband. Kleenex boxes and bars of soap he took
from the hospital which never appreciated him. He did so much,
she tells me, and how his physical therapy patients
loved him. But she took out the garden,

his garden, where she pulled up the wrong things
by the roots on purpose. *That's the only way you could
win with Henry,* she tells me. The children don't hear any of this;
they are finishing their second piece of birthday cake,
and we want to get them out of here, before
they break something. We back the truck
down the driveway. Her face fades inside
the thick shock of white hair and the fog print
made by her breath, blurring into a small sticker, a price tag
on the window of the house hugged by pines.

Sparrow

One morning she wakes to find herself
one of them.
She learns the value
of camouflage. How to build
with the salvage
of gardens, kite string, dryer lint.
Fights her way to feeders
stocked for those more beautiful,
refusing to be driven off
by cardinals, jays,
nuthatches. In winter,
she puffs herself, clamps
onto pine branch.
She wakes easily.
Her hunger is fierce.
Her bones,
hollow for flight.
Her heart of feathers.

At the Cemetery
on the Twentieth Anniversary
of My Mother's Death

I do not know why I have stayed away
all these years, nor what is left here.

At morning Mass, advice in the epistle:
Let the dead bury the dead. And lately

I've been thinking about trees—
cedar, maple, paper birch—how inside,

they render themselves numb,
one wrapped layer over another,

making heartwood; how
every year my hands

look more and more like hers.
In the backyard I plant plump

hips of tulips—ruffled pink Parrot,
red Darwin, yellow Bellona,

her favorite—in beds, twist each one
into earth. As benediction,

I sprinkle bone meal, like ashes,
like breath in winter air.

Conversations with My Mother

1.
She can hear the sponge mop
from her chair in the living room.
I am home, taking vacation time
to clean her house, wash
her hair, which falls out
in my lathered hands.

The exasperation in her voice
reaches me in her kitchen:
You don't seem to understand, she says. *I*
am dying. You know
how that floor should be done.

The bubbles in the bucket blink at me—
they don't know either
whether to laugh or cry.
Mom, I say, *I do understand.*
Getting down on my knees won't
change it.

2.
She prayed the Hail Mary
mother to mother
out loud.
Holy Mary, Mother of God,
pray for us sinners now
and at the hour of our death.
I mean it. Amen.

3.
On the TV bolted to the wall
the game show audience
applauds. *What did I win?* she asks me.
Her eyes are shut. She is
becoming smaller than the print
on her hospital gown. I whisper
my answer. We both
go home.

What Happened
at My Bird Feeder

*[Life] is the little shadow which runs across
the grass and loses itself in the sunset.*
CROWFOOT

What a small wild thing it is,
happiness. There on the ground,

among the cracked shells of sunflowers,
discrete splats of blood startle the snow.

It was a quick, clean kill, like January.
Leaning close, I see with surprise

that the snowflakes have kept their shape,
their intricate lace now dyed

an improbable red. Above me,
the sparrows seek refuge in pine trees—

green monks with sleeves full of fragrance,
their hooded faces distant, lost in prayer.

If they saw, they do not say. The sky,
pink with the brief beat of sunset,

throbs against the lull of white,
blue gray, branch brown,

the slow accumulation of grief.

Neutrinos and the
Unified Theory

Sometimes I can almost
forget it's there, the loss,
once a knot the size of a child's fist

wedged up under my rib cage,
but breaking up now, more
like neutrinos—

billions of them, smaller than atoms,
than electrons, hatched
in the hearts of stars

to blow through us
as though we were windows,
thrown open on a spring day.

I am as bad as the scientists.
I want to explain everything
but cannot devise an experiment

as ingenious as theirs,
this plan to fire the tiny particles
457 miles underground, from Chicago

to northern Minnesota, aim them
at a neutrino detector
in an abandoned mine.

What is there for me to prove?
The scientists will count
how many neutrinos show up,

and rejoice at the ones who don't.
These will be not lost, but transformed—
proof that neutrinos have mass

and what looks like emptiness
in the universe is the answer
to the whole

equation.

Laws of Falling Things

Gravity points to the center of things.
Family scars, the heart's footprint.
This is the direction called down.
I fled to the willow, it loved me back,

my family scars, my heart's footprint,
restless in the switch and sway
of girlhood, swooning branches, a waterfall
of leaf and light. I was practicing wildness,

restless in the switch and sway,
the air—who knew it could slow you down?
Bodies fall straight to still water,
the pond that claimed the willow years later.

The air—who knew it could slow you down?
—must have roared up suddenly
to split the trunk, half standing, half trapped
in ice. I wasn't there, didn't hear the crack.

It must have roared up suddenly, the sound
falling upward, against the rules,
no mass for gravity to seize.
Now an uneven scar on the hill, my sorrow

falling upward, against the rules,
the way all things fall side by side
in a vacuum, no air to slow you down, only grief
whose gravity points to the center of things.

The Delirium of Swiftness

We struggle to understand just how they did it—
the temperatures approaching absolute zero,
cold past all endurance, atoms clinging together,
almost motionless, molasses for the laser,
enough to slow the speed of light by a factor
of twenty million, to only thirty-eight miles an hour.
The Heisenberg uncertainty principle,
which I take to mean that the only way
to know where you are
is to be still, except of course you can't
really do that; we're all rafting
on the water table, the earth's crust
spinning at such a clip that if it stopped
we'd all hurtle eastward at 800 miles an hour.
That would be momentum. Heisenberg says
the faster we go, the more uncertain
our location, and I think he must be talking
about infatuation, how we race
to lives we weren't planning on
and don't recognize when we get them.
Just think, it was only a century ago
the doctors were warning people
the new sport of bicycling could bring on
the delirium of swiftness,
give you a haggard bicycle face,
from the strain of keeping the machine
upright. Now we have a new millennium
and a new machine, making light so slow
a bicyclist could overtake it.
Blame Einstein. I had forgotten
that light slows down every day
for transparent things: water,
diamonds, my face
looking for yours, glass.

To My Husband
on Our Anniversary

It bothers me, not to know
its name, that gangly tree
they took down on the boulevard.

I swept sawdust off the sidewalk,
touched the moist blond rings,
counted twenty-five years, some of them fat.
I found the soft brown rot.

All we knew then was exterior:
every spring a little slower to leaf out,
more bare branches, and then the storm
yanking the largest branch

like an arm out of its socket.
I am relieved to be rid of it
and ashamed of how we stood by,
watched a thing go slowly bad.

All around us, trees felled by wind.
We have to tend the marriage
every day.

Family Reunion

Past the barn, past the worm-ridden apple trees,
two pheasants gawk around a fat roll of hay.
The apples are gone now, to the children and the deer,
and the trees are bored. They stand on their heads,
roots upended, leaves underground. The oaks

have gone copper, too stubborn to let go.
Which side of the family gave the birches
their red hair? From across the field
their pale, thin bodies stand out
against the poplars and scrub maple,
like white sprouting in a beard. The pines

came early, sucked up all the green
and hold it, tart with sap, in their throats.
All along the freeway, Norways
wait in line patiently, hum softly
so the babies can nap. Standing apart,

the jack pines are scrappy, boastful.
The tamaracks hide by the swamp,
shamefaced—cross-dressers,
caught in the act—bare of needles
in dead of winter. The blue spruce,

vain about their figures,
dangle pinecone charm bracelets.
And the patriarch, the lanky white pine,
with branches like Moses,
parting the Red Sea, gathers the tribe,
wind-drawn, and leads the grace.

Lifesaving

They did not, in the end,
pump my stomach,
but they kept me overnight,
and if anyone yelled at me
for sipping what I thought
was Coca-Cola
from an hourglass bottle
in my friend's garage,
while her brother's feet stuck out
from under the Chevrolet,
I do not remember it. Surely
my father told them
I was smart enough
to spit out gasoline.

What I remember
is the indignity
of being put back into a crib
when I had a big bed at home.
I remember how high
the ceiling seemed
when you looked up,
and that someone else
in the hospital nursery,
someone littler and more afraid,
was crying. And I stood
in the dark and called out, *It's okay.*

Don't cry. And I remember
the new doll my mother brought me,
and the doctor telling my father
they could take me home.
What I can't remember
is how I came
to be rowing my mother
around the pond behind our house.

I cannot keep her in the boat.
Over and over I pull her back in,
dripping, until finally
she slips away.

I never remember
seeing her swim.
It was my father who taught me,
his hand under my back,
his face a beacon smiling, *This way,*
this way—
a way out
of my mother, who watched
from behind the long
grass of her fear,
her unhappiness pale,
unstoppable as the springs
that filled the pond.

Maternal Instinct

Filled with the sudden
unlikely pleasure of being
in my own house
in the middle of the afternoon,
sun streaming in, a pile of clean shirts,
the simplicity of an ironing board.
My glorious firstborn,
his long predictable nap.
Me humming, watching TV—
something mindless—
making plans and sliding the iron
back and forth. Until—did he cry out?
I realize that I have,
for the first time since his birth,
momentarily but completely
forgotten him.

～

Her face lit by the monitor's glow,
fingers poised over keys
in home position, my daughter types
her fourth-grade play,
sings along to the country
station. She has all the heartaches
memorized. Like this one,
with a mother worried about
her unmarried daughter,
that All the Good Ones
Are Gone—
But what I hear
is the mother's lie—
I only want what's best for you—
the lie I heard, the lie
I will surely tell.

～

Two mothers, we share
the porch. Me on my side
with rocker and notebook,
she on hers, fierce in a neat
hollow of grass and mud,

hidden behind the straw wreath
hung next to the door.
When she flies off,
I peer in:
one tiny white egg.

That afternoon the children
tear in after school, yelling for help—
the sparrow's neck is tangled in a string,
and she is dangling from the wreath,
alternately flapping, and going
limp. I lift her with my palm,
and she shakes free, takes off.
The next day, a second egg,
but the bird never returns.
Is this nature's intention?

I send the abandoned nest
to an artist friend in the city,
a sculpture of dryer lint
and bent grass.

In Certain Slavic Legends

there are as many
as seven winds. How many kinds
of light? Even Claude Monet
couldn't paint them all, though
he lined up canvasses in front of
the field, the pond, the garden,
and moved from one to the next
as the light changed. I wonder
if he knew by looking which
was ten o'clock and which two,
the way the Inuit are intimate with snow:
Qanik if the snow is falling,
but *isiriataq* if it's falling yellow
or red, and *qanniapaluk* if falling
lightly in still air. On the ground
it's *aputi,* though if it's a thin snow
coating an object, *piirturiniq.*
In English, we're forced to improvise:
the tree-sticking kind that comes late
in the season, the kind that swirls
the hood of the car at intersections,
the kind your boots punch through.
Angry sideways-falling snow, or the kind
that falls every which way,
as though it were having so much fun dancing
it forgot all about the ground.
The kind that piles so high
you don't recognize places you've been
every day of your life, like love—
another word we all use
but whose music is far richer
and more intricate
than we can ever say.

For Mike and LeAnn

Over Greenland

Cramped inside walls curved
like the planet below,
we track the sun homeward,
never questioning the implausible
numbers on the washed-out
screen at the front of the cabin:
423 miles an hour, 32,000 feet
altitude above a misnamed
continent, a drab biscuit,
crumpled and pocked,
like the skin of a napping
grandaunt seen at too close
range, above the weather,
above consequence, clouds
scudding below, their shadows huge,
hurried footprints on the landscape,
bold impermanence, and there,
barely moving, our tiny
shape, like a balsa wood model
a boy gets for Christmas,
wings, tail, fuselage,
no inkling of the equations
keeping us aloft.
We squint, unable
to look away.

Three

Rapid Eye Movement

*Eugene Aserinsky, 77, a scientist who
discovered rapid eye movement sleep,
died Wednesday after his car veered
off the road and crashed into a tree.*
NEWSPAPER OBITUARY, JULY 30, 1998

1.
Do we conclude the car
was at fault, or the tree,
for not moving?
Maybe the old man
played all the parts:
driver, car, tree.
That's how it is
in dreams. The car
is looking for the tree.
The tree is waiting
for the car. The driver
protests his innocence.

2.
The light switched off hours ago,
the glass of water on the nightstand
already gone stale.
Ignore the legs
scissoring beneath the sheets,
the quickening breath.
See the eyes, how they twitch
behind thin curtains.

3.
Seen from the car,
the trees
surge past, gaunt
marathoners.
Some in groups,
others straggling.
This must be mile 22.
A few seize up on the sidelines,
collapse in the ditch.

4.

Lately my dreams
repeat. That house that spirals
into the ground. Barn owls
blinking on our alley garage.
All the creatures
peacefully giving birth
in the closets and stairwells
of our house:
cats, squirrels, mink,
every night more of them.

5.

Scrubwomen of the air,
all day hauling water from root
to leaf. When a child climbs too high
and falls, nobody blames
hard ground. It's trees
they accuse—of blocking views,
dropping leaves, choking grass
with shade. That incident
with the hiker and the lightning.
Now these two moons shrieking
out of the dark.

6.

According to myth, green trees
shelter the dead. In winter,
the spirits of drowned maidens
prefer the cool Danube.
But when the sun
climbs summer's road, they escape
to shimmy up birch and willow,
swing the branches.

7.
The dreaming mind vibrates
at the same frequency as the earth.
Each night the mind climbs eagerly
into the boat, paddles as if to leave
the body of water.

On these waves come bobbing
coded ransom notes from the soul,
messages smuggled back to the dreamer,
who in the morning, disbelieves.

Audition for a Love Poem

Your hand on my hip, a slow rudder
as we round the bend of sleep.

On the phone, your voice
in the middle of the day,
a tug on the fishing line.

Your eyes in the photograph,
locked on mine, straight through
the lens, over the oblivious,
curly head of our son,
a toddler pointing
to the book in your lap.

Smaller than that.
The sound
of my name on your lips—
Those two
particular syllables rising
up through your throat,
over tongue, teeth, lips.
I overhear you talking
to someone else at a party,
feel the vibration of my name
rolling outward.
Say it again.

How Things Sound

1.

The sound designer says he drives in thinking about it, whether
a little more wind would be better. It's eerie to watch the film
before he does his work, before he goes out with a tape
recorder, thieving sounds from roadsides of other days. He lays
them down gently to paste in later, one oscillating wave at a time.
He starts with how it would have been before we got here—
maybe how it is now, without us—no soles of shoes chafing grit,
no trees clearing leafy throats, no feathers stroking air.

We watch the scene again, this time with sound. He tells us the
flapping of the raven's wings is really the nylon cover of an old
JVC recorder, snapping the air in front of the microphone.

2.

The male cricket serenades with his wings.
His love music trembles up her front legs.

3.

A sound is a narrow stretch of water between two places, deep
and protected.
A sound is nothing but a wave, a vibration, until it reaches an
ear—a boat launched only when it reaches the shore. Air is a
slow soup.
A sound moves four times faster through water, faster still
through steel.
A sound is like the rest of us—it spreads out around corners
and the edges of things, tries to prepare for the unexpected.
A sound changing speed is a sound changing direction, like I
am now.

I know this worries you, and sound that is bending is harder
to hear. Like a dream, a sound travels farther at night and
fades with the dawn. I listen hard to dreams, but hear only wind
racing over gray grass. I call out to you, my voice nothing but
air rushing over vocal cords. So I pile words of reassurance into
paper boats and push them across this stretch of water. Has no
one told you? It's the nature of sound to race after light.

4.

Just off U.S. Highway 71 in Redwood Falls, gold-fringed streamers run out from the Tom Thumb store to the gas pumps. The wind can't leave them alone. I close my eyes and hear the chatter of poplars above northern lakes, poplars worried about being struck dumb. They've heard rumors of loggers, and newsprint— the slurry of pulp, the stamping of ink, columns of words silent as moon.

The wood in a violin ripples a full day after it is played. This is why mothers stand nightly over cribs and whisper, *I love you, I love you*—

5.

At dinner one night my son announces he'd rather be a unicorn. We nod, clink silverware on our plates. Who wouldn't want a magic horn? Plus, unicorns don't have to go to school. But my son also envies their elegant unicorn language, many leaps above the crude tongues of humans.

Snorting, hissing, my son takes on the voices of animals, roars to terrorize his sister. When finally I can't stand the racket, I make my voice steely, and hurl it up the stairs: *Hey! You may not eat your sister!* There is a moment of silence, and then, plaintive: *Not even her hand?*

6.

The researchers who track these things tell us the brain is a union shop. When I read this to myself in *Time* magazine, one set of neurons switches on. But they flip off and another set tingles when I read aloud to you. And your neurons, which dance to receive my words, freeze and wait for others to toss the same words back aloud.

The scientists are still clocking the speed of sounds, like fastballs and speedboats. Hard consonants fly by at forty milliseconds each, but the vowels resonate for one hundred milliseconds, sometimes more. Without the vowels, the consonants collide. The vowels make the spaces where the meaning comes in.

When I move on, become a sound, let me be vowel, quivering in the air.

How Time Works

He would sit sometimes at the kitchen table
over a dinner plate bare except for a pile of beets
or a plop of creamed corn
and listen to the rest of the family outside,
his parents scritching rakes and talking
to neighbors, his sister creaking the porch swing.
He'd watch the open-faced clock over the door
pull the light from the window over the sink,
drag it across the linoleum, pushing it finally
down the hall to the back closet
which held his baseball mitt and skates.
      He wondered if this
was what time did. His mother seemed to think
it knew how to fly, but no one had pictures.
His father was always looking for wherever time
had gone, was fond of saying, "Time's a-wastin'!"
as if it were an ice cream cone
that would run down your fist if you didn't
lick fast enough.
      The boy suspected
that time lived in boxes that grownups
kept track of, boxes labeled according to what you
were supposed to be doing: time to wash up,
time to come in, time for bed. Clearly time
had the power to boss you around.
      It ticked at you,
like the old clock on the mantel in the front room.
Once, when they left him home from Sunday services
he climbed up and got it down. He pried off the back
with his father's screwdriver, excited to see at last
how time works. With its brass heart beating in his hands,
he ran across the street and up the aisle to his family's pew,
but his parents did not seem to understand.
His mother marched him home and cried
in front of the fireplace.
      For his punishment,
his father made him sit in a dining room chair
for an hour, hands out, palms facing each other,
a string laid across the top. He'd seen his father's
hands this way, a skein of yarn draped over them,

while his mother wrapped the wool
around and around, into balls,
each one a round, worsted hour
she'd make into mittens, hats,
something he would lose
and never get back.

The Patience of Grass

While cleaning the basement, my son
brings me a jar of grass seed,
drab slivers left over
from last year's experiment
planted in a pot tied in raffia,
a centerpiece for the New Year's table.
It sat, a shock of green on linen,
alarmed no doubt at the blank
white world outside the window,
the embarrassing nakedness
of branches. I shake the Mason jar,
roll it over next to my ear,
hear the wind rise and fall.
I think of the seed art at the state fair,
picture someone sitting at a kitchen table
in the late afternoon, patiently
laying seeds in place with a tweezers
—gluing in kernels of corn,
sunflower seeds, pale beans,
each a full belly. And the grains,
stitches in a painstaking embroidery,
scenes of farm buildings,
churning brooks, muscular clouds
holding back all that sky
and at night, stars
baking in a blue oven.

Only All the Time

It's like having something inside you that will die,
is dying,
but at the same time is stretching, a green gymnastic thing,
doing somersaults and tumbling,
       like a vine,
            like kudzu,
that grabs whatever it can to pull itself up and hangs onto anything,
eager,
delighted almost
at an obstacle, something to go over or around:
       a fence,
            the garage,
entire neighborhoods even,
until you are completely leafed over, helpless, unable to see
anything else,
and there is no point in denying it, you are consumed now
with photosynthesis,
and when he asks if you've been thinking about him, you
don't say anything
but there it is,
coursing its athletic heat,
your answer,
that truth.

Late June

Rivers sleep like children—
on their backs, murmuring at the moon.

Nights when the wind will not quit teasing
the moon goes to pieces on the water.

Fish come up and nibble the gleam.

Say It Was a Dream the River Had

1.
Trees will always take me in,
but the river has heard all my lines before.
I want to ride her somewhere, but my plan

involves a raft, a canoe, paddles
dripping an arc as they return. The river
has other plans: a tug I cannot

resist, the swoop and swallow of cold
along the bottom, until I am face-to-face
with a long trail of stones tossed

years ago. My cheeks hollow, begin
to feel gill-like. Soon, one bubble at a time,
the very idea of air escapes me.

What counts now is how
danger reveals itself—in shape,
in movement and light.

2.
We'd go bent-legged down the hill
to the pond, poke hooks through bologna,
cast and wait. Not that we really wanted
the fish. A tug was real enough.
Anyway the fishing ended
when Kimberly Peltier caught a fishhook
in her cheek, and our mothers
took away the hooks. Bored but unwilling
to abandon the only mystery we could swim in,
we'd shred Wonder Bread for the ducks,
fat white ducks we'd once lured up into the yard
with a trail of crumbs and chased
into the street, shrieking, the ducks frantic,
squawking, wings flailing,
cruelty pounding in our hearts.

3.
He caught it in a jar with markings
on the side to measure how much had fallen.
Three quarters of an inch, he'd say,
Pretty good, as if the rain cared
what he thought. She always said

the best rain falls at night, intent
on the roof. Man and wife,
they sleep now inside
this sound, sink through layers
of silver scales, unblinking dream
eyes on the sides of their heads
fixed on flickers of black and white.

Well, are you surprised?
he demands. *This is what happens
when you build too close
to the river; the streams
tunnel right under your house.*
But she insists she needs the sound
of water to sleep. At first

she's not sure where
the water is. She senses
something is there
but stalls
until the rug gets wet.
Finally she drags the bed away,
peels back the rug,
pries up the floorboards.
She stays that way
lying on her stomach
staring into the fallow
parts of herself until dawn.

4.
I had gotten separated from the others.
It was dark and the aquarium lit
so everything was rinsed green
save the fish, like gaudy Pucci scarves,
darting silk with war-painted faces.
Their stares, the undulation of whisker
and gill, unnerved me. I pressed
fingers to glass: proof the danger
was walled up and even lost children
cannot slip easily through glass.

5.
You go to the trouble of laying a foundation,
you expect it to stay put.

> *Say the dream was not your house pitching in the waves.*

You do not expect the toss and roll, a fish
who warns you: Hold on. Hold still.

> *Say you watched the whole thing from the shore,*
> *absentmindedly poking a stick in the sand.*

You do not expect to find yourself sitting on the bottom,
leaning first one way and then another, like seaweed,
unconcerned.

A Poster in the
Cloquet Forestry Center

tells us:
Black bears in northern forests
eat the fruit and flowering
of planted things:
red oak acorns,
catkins and young leaves of aspen,
wild sarsaparilla,
blueberries, strawberries,
peavine, juneberries,
pincherry, hazelnut,
blue joint grass, interrupted
fern.
    I wonder
what it was doing
when it was interrupted.
And is it shocked, or
does the fern wait
for this, for the slice of sharp teeth,
the bath of saliva on mottled tongue?

Long Division

Day squeezes itself
into a crack, and we
crawl around inside it
on our bellies, pretending
that what has become usual
is normal. This is December,

squinting, then startled
by January, a mountain
looking for planes to bully.
Launched on a dare,
we fly by feel and the scent
of danger at ten o'clock,
stunt pilots following a line
in the air. Finally in February,

though we still live close,
sap stirs the pin oak,
whose leaves tumble brown,
dry cereal in winter's bowl.
We cannot yet see
over the rim. But the sun
is starting to remember things—

its own face reflected in the bay,
unclenching clods of earth,
the gratitude of grass,
sunflowers craning necks
to follow light across a day

—all this is coming back, and the sun
resolves to try harder. We
do likewise, steel ourselves
against too much hope. March comes

in rivulets, and we row
upstream into the afterwinter,
happy even for the rough
knuckles of Lent, willing
to do penance, anything
to seed our clear-cut hearts,
resume nature's confident
multiplication. We yearn to touch
again the skin of what is easy,
make of winter a dream,
a snow dome, in the palm
of the hand.

Going to the Car Wash
Early, in a Fog

Cars and trucks, cardboard cutouts
pulled on slow strings past buildings floating
without faces, without
feet. The streetlights,
a rosary she prays
to get through this dream
the city is having. She drives,
as if in tissue paper,
an unopened present. It's worth it,

this winter dawn drive—only one car
ahead of her. She follows
commands: DRIVE FORWARD.
STOP. And she tries to. She sits
under the furious suds,
the pummeling brushes,
and practices not looking back
at the thing she has resolved
to let go. But she knows
she is cheating. Secretly
she hopes God will press it back
into her hands, say,
No, really, I wanted you to have this.

Emerging as if from the confessional
her car comes clean.
Dissolving in the swirl, the street salt
rides the water down, positive
and negative ions releasing,
leaping, in the belly of the fog.

RONALD H REIMANN, SR
6100 Hadley Avenue South
Cottage Grove, Minnesota 55016-1027

22 June 2000

Dear Joe and Carolyn,

Perhaps you think poetry came from another era and has little to do with your life. But if beauty and romance has a role in your lives together, then I think your marriage would benefit from making time for good verse.

These poems are from a long-time friend, the wife of a former railroad colleague. I hope that you will devote part of a relaxed evening, and read some of these aloud to one another. Take the time to enjoy the words and the meaning. Feel the passion and the fun in the words. Enjoy the beauty and depth of these ideas and her language.

Love,

Dad

A M
D G

651-459-0317
OckhamRaz@wavetech.net

What Appears Wanting

All she has to do
is announce at dinner
she is going to work on a poem, then go
into her office and shut the door.
 Her son will appear,
wanting to be quizzed
on methods of transportation
in Spanish: *en motocicleta, a caballero, a pie.*
 Her daughter will appear,
wanting Mom's reaction to the horse
she pines for now: a brown Morgan,
white heart on the forehead.
 Her husband will appear,
wanting company on a walk. And though she
is lonely for herself,
 she cannot resist
the moon on fresh snow, the possibility
of woodsmoke in his hair
on the pillow.
 The walks, unshoveled
this late in the season,
the lit windows
of other people's lives:
music open on a piano, the fluttering blue
scarf of television in a living room.
 From the alley,
a kitchen table set with one white plate—
a tangerine, partially peeled,
a chair pushed back,
the clock's blank face,
 Buddha on the wall.

Early Evening in the Kitchen of Love

Love is always stirring and
thinking about what it will do.
ST. TERESA OF ÁVILA

The light runs
in through the window
like somebody's chasing it.
Her hair is all wild,
and she hums
and dances a little,
with those hips of hers,
serious hips, good for toting
babies, or propping open
the screen door
while she calls me
down from the backyard tree.

And this is the call
I've been waiting for,
this is what I want to know:
what Love's been fixing
for me. So I push
into her kitchen,
stand on tiptoes,
try to see
what she's got
in that big pot of hers.
Is goodness
something the mouth
can decide?

Years later, the smell
is almost an ache,
the downdraft
of left-behind dreams.

I stand
facing the stove
a long time.
I stir and wait,
hoping
to catch the secret
sleeping in the low
afternoon,
wake it
steaming
in the valley
of my spoon.

Prairie Meditations

Watching the real thing, we marvel.
They had it all worked out. The wind
would take the seeds of grasses
under its wing, introduce them around.
Bluestem, short wheat, buffalo—
luring the wind on a long legged romp,
laughing and tripping, a tumble of stalks and bloom.
City grass barely remembers this.
It colors inside the margins
of sidewalks and bows to lawnmower blades.
The lure of unflappable prairie,
an open palm, is a surprise.

From the passenger seat I trace lifelines
on a map, county roads linking towns
I know only from winter school closing announcements:
Storedon-Jeffers, Butterfield-Odin, Windom:
Two hours late, and no morning kindergarten. Buses
on plowed roads only. I imagine snowsuited children
cheering, bursting out of houses that hunched
close together, houses wincing, waiting
for the rolling pin wind to bear down.

But this is summer. We are taking the kids to see
an outdoor prairie pageant, to sleep in a sod house.
This horizon, a gift they must unwrap themselves.
Beside us, power lines, like a musical staff
and above, a pair of red-winged blackbirds swoop,
a musical slur in the sky. A deer
lopes unevenly through alfalfa.

Looking for the petroglyphs at Jeffers, we overshoot
and double back, wade through grass
to where stone like God's cheekbone
rises from the flat, thrust upward in some
wrenching cataclysm and left to bake
in the sun. If Emerson is right, and prayer
is contemplation of the facts from the highest
point of view, this is a temple. I kneel, trace my fingers
in ancient carvings: thunderbirds, turtles,
stone stories of hunts and journeys.

We think the prairie has been waiting for us,
but grass has its own agenda.
If some part of your heart is buried here,
the prairie does not care. At a museum in Pipestone
we're reminded: the clay settled here first.

Prairie unfurls inside me, teaching this:
The wind has all the time in the world.
The sky goes on without you.
Do what grasses do: keep thick
your connections underground.
Then it's all right to give yourself over to fire.
You'll grow back from the base, surging
from strong jolt of ash, grow into the wind
headlong and blazing.

Acknowledgments

The following poems, or versions of them, have appeared in these publications:

"Swim the Night" in *ArtWord Quarterly,* no. 6 (Fall 1996);

"Madalyn Murray O'Hair May Never Come Back" in *Deepbreath,* an on-line magazine published by Winona State University (December 1996);

"Prairie Meditations" in *Mankato Poetry Review* (May 1997);

"Conversations with My Mother" and "Visiting Aunt Dorothy on Her Birthday" in *North Coast Review,* no. 11 (Fall/Winter 1996);

"November Sleeping" in *Sidewalks,* no. 11 (Fall/Winter 1996/1997), "What Happened at My Bird Feeder" and "Empty Nest" in *Sidewalks,* no. 13 (Fall/Winter 1997/1998), and "Over Greenland" in *Sidewalks,* no. 17 (Fall/Winter 1999/2000);

"In Defense of Semicolons" in *Wolfhead Quarterly,* 4, no. 4 (Autumn 1998);

"Going to the Car Wash Early, in a Fog" appeared in the *1998 Minnesota Poetry Calendar,* "Widow" appeared in the *1999 Minnesota Poetry Calendar,* and "At the Cemetery on the Twentieth Anniversary of My Mother's Death" appeared in the *2000 Minnesota Poetry Calendar;*

"Implosion" was published in *A Definitive Guide to the Twin Cities* (St. Paul: Spout Press, 1997);

"Audition for a Love Poem" and "Rapid Eye Movement" appeared in *Writing the Wave,* an anthology of winning manuscripts from the Lake Superior Writers' Contest '99 (November 1999);

"Spiders Keep House" appears in the anthology *Essential Love: Poems about Mothers and Fathers, Daughters and Sons* (West Hartford, Conn.: Grayson Books, 2000).

I'd also like to thank the very kind and talented Tom Andrews for the first line of "Family Reunion," taken from his poem "Dr. Farnsworth, a Chiropodist, Lived in Ohio, Where He Wrote Only the First Lines of Poems," from his book, *The Brother's Country* (New York: Persea Books, 1990). "Only All the Time" took its title and syntax from "Part of Eve's Discussion," by Marie Howe, from her book *The Good Thief* (New York: Persea Books, 1988). Jaime Meyer graciously consented to use of the quotation that appears with "Grammar in the Kingdom of God."

So many people have helped shape the poems in this book, and I am grateful for the opportunity to thank them: my fellow students and teachers at the Loft, an organization devoted to helping writers and supporting literature, especially John Reinhard; my editor at New Rivers Press, Connie Wanek; and fellow poets Becca Barniskis, Kath Jesme, Amy McNamara, and Mary Jo Thompson.

Finally, I would like to thank Chris Welsh, whose love and support make amazing things possible.

Susan Steger Welsh lives with her husband and
two children in St. Paul, Minnesota, where she
works as a writer. Her work has appeared in
several anthologies and literary journals, and
she was awarded first place for poetry in the
1999 Lake Superior Writers' Contest. Welsh is
also the recipient of a Minnesota State Arts
Board Fellowship for 2000. *Rafting on the Water
Table* is her first book.